Basic Principles

of

Monastic Spirituality

Basic
Principles
of
Monastic
Spirituality

Thomas Merton

TEMPLEGATE PUBLISHERS

Templegate Publishers
302 East Adams Street
P.O. Box 5152
Springfield, Illinois
62705
(217) 522-3353

ISBN 0-87243-222-X
Library of Congress Catalog Card Number:
96-60151
Cover photograph by John Howard Griffin
© 1996 by Elizabeth Griffin-Bonazzi

CONTENTS

Foreword

FOREWORD

There can be no doubt that the monastic vocation is one of the most beautiful in the Church of God. The "contemplative life," as the life of the monastic orders is usually called today, is a life entirely devoted to the mystery of Christ, to living the life of God who gives Himself to us in Christ. It is a life totally abandoned to the Holy Spirit, a life of humility, obedience, solitude, silence, prayer, in which we renounce our own desires and our own ways in order to live in the liberty of the sons of God, guided by the Holy Spirit speaking through our Superiors, our Rule, and in the inspirations of His grace within our hearts. It is a life of total self-oblation to God, in union with Jesus who was crucified for us and rose from the dead and lives in us by His Holy Spirit.

But beautiful as this life may be, simple and exalted as the tradition of the monastic Fathers may show it to us, monks are human and human frailty tends always to diminish and to distort the wholeness of what is given to us by God. This is all the more to be regretted when some souls full of good will and generosity embrace the monastic life, only to find their good will dissipated in futilities and in routine. Instead of living the monastic life in its purity and simplicity, we always tend to complicate it or to pervert it with our own limited views and our own too human desires. We place exaggerated emphasis on some partial aspect of the life, thus unbalancing the whole. Or we fall into that spiritual myopia which sees nothing but details and loses sight of the great organic unity in which we are called to live. In a word, if the countless rules and observances of the monastic life are to be properly understood, we must always keep in view the real meaning of monasticism. In order not to be confused by the means which are given to us, we must always relate them to their end.

The great ends of the monastic life can only be seen in the light of the mystery of Christ. Christ is the center of monastic living. He is its source and its end. He is the way of the monk as well as his goal. Monastic rules and observances, the practices of monastic asceticism and prayer, must always be integrated in this higher reality. They must always be seen as part of a living reality, as manifestations of a *divine life* rather than as elements in a system, as manifestations of duty alone. The monk does more than conform to edicts and commands which he cannot understand — he abandons his will in order to live in Christ. He renounces a lower freedom for a higher one. But if this renunciation is to be fruitful and valid, the monk must have some idea of what he is doing.

The purpose of these notes is to examine briefly the great theological principles without which monastic observance and monastic life would have no meaning. The truth we present here must necessarily take a very condensed form. Anyone who wishes to understand them must read them meditatively and in the presence of God.

Although these pages have been written for monks, and in particular for Cistercian novices and postulants, they will have meaning for all religious and indeed for all Christians, since the monastic life is traditionally regarded as the pure Christian life, the perfect life "in Christ," a sure way to the summit of that ordinary perfection of charity to which Jesus has called all those who have left the world to follow Him to heaven.

I

Whom Do You Seek?

If we want to live as monks, we must try
to understand what the monastic life really is. We must try to reach the springs
from which that life flows. We must have
some notion of our spiritual roots, that
we may be better able to sink them deep
into the soil.

But the monastic vocation is a mystery. Therefore it cannot be completely
expressed in a clear succinct formula. It
is a gift of God, and we do not understand
it as soon as we receive it, for all God's
gifts, especially His spiritual gifts, share
in His own hiddenness and in His own
mystery. God will reveal Himself to us

in the gift of our vocation, but He will do this only gradually.

We can expect to spend our whole lives as monks entering deeper and deeper into the mystery of our monastic vocation, which is our life hidden with Christ in God. If we are real monks, we are constantly rediscovering what it means to be a monk, and yet we never exhaust the full meaning of our vocation.

When we enter the monastery, we may or may not have some notion why we have left the world. We can give some answer, more or less clear, to the question: "Why have you come here?" This question is one which we should ask ourselves again and again in the course of our monastic life; "What are you doing here? Why have you come here?" Not that it is a question whose answer we have known but tend to forget. It is a question which confronts us with a new meaning and a new urgency, as we go on in life.

Sometimes we hesitate to ask ourselves this question, afraid that by doing so we might shake the foundations of our vocation. The question is one which ought never to be evaded. If we face it seriously, we will strengthen our vocation. If we evade it, even under a holy pretext, we may perhaps allow our vocation to be undermined.

The monk who ceases to ask himself "Why have you come here?" has perhaps ceased to be a monk.

What are some of the answers to give to the question: "Why have you come here?" We reply — "To save my soul," "To lead a life of prayer," "To do penance for my sins," "To give myself to God," "To love God." These are good enough answers. They are religious answers. They are meaningful not only for what they say, but for what they imply.

15

For, on the lips of a Christian, such statements must eventually mean much more than they actually say. As they stand, they give evidence of good subjective dispositions, but they by no means lead to a full understanding of the monastic life. For the monastic life is not defined merely by the fact that it enables us to save our soul, to pray, to do penance, to love God. All these things can be done outside the monastery and *are* done by thousands.

But neither is Christian monasticism adequately defined as a quest of perfection. A Zen buddhist, in Japan, for example, may enter a monastery to seek a life of retirement and spiritual discipline. He is perhaps seeking the highest reality. He is seeking "liberation." Now if we enter the monastery seeking the highest reality, seeking perfection, we must nevertheless realize that for us this means something somewhat more than it can ever mean for a Zen buddhist.

Our monastic life must therefore develop so that our concept of the end for which we are striving becomes more clearly and more specifically Christian.

It makes much more sense to say, as St. Benedict says, that we come to the monastery to *seek God,* than to say that we come seeking spiritual perfection.

The end which we seek is not merely something within ourselves, some personal quality added to ourselves, some new gift. It is God Himself.

To say "Why have you come here?" is the same as saying "What does it mean, to seek God? How do you know if you are seeking Him or not? How can you tell the difference between seeking Him and not seeking Him, when He is in fact a hidden God, *Deus absconditus?*"

When Moses spoke to God saying: "Show me thy face" the Lord answered, "Man shall not see me and live." (Exodus 33:20.)

Yet Jesus tells us that eternal life is to know the one true God, and Jesus Christ whom He has sent. (John 17:3.) This knowledge of God which is eternal life is not arrived at by pure speculation. We come to know God by being born of God and living in God. We cannot really know Him only by reading and study and meditation.

We can come to know God only by becoming His sons and living as His sons. "As many as received Him, He gave the power to be made sons of God, to them that believe in His name, who are born not of blood, nor of the will of the flesh, nor of the will of man, but of God." (John I:12-13.)

We can live as sons of God, we can know God only if we live in charity.

"Dearly beloved, let us love one another, for charity is of God. And every one that loveth is born of God, and knoweth God." (I John 4:7.)

But this charity is not just a natural love for one another. We do not become sons of God by the mere fact of living together in a society dedicated to a common purpose, sharing common interests with one another. Do not even the Gentiles so? The charity that unites us is the charity of Christ — in the strict sense of a love *exercised* by the Sacred Heart, not just as the broad sense of a love patterned on His love. We sing at the *Mandatum* — *congregavit nos in unum Christi amor* — the love of Christ's Heart for us (not just our love for Him) has drawn us together. We could not love Him unless "He had first loved us."

We become sons of God by being born again in Christ — by baptism — and we live and grow and bring forth fruit only by "remaining in Christ."

"Abide in me and I in you. As the branch cannot bear fruit of itself unless it abide in the vine, so neither can you

unless you abide in me." (John 15:4.)
Thus we arrive at the real heart of our
monastic vocation.

Our monastic life is a life in Christ, a
life by which we remain in Christ, sharing His life, participating in His action,
united with Him in His worship of the
Father.

Christ is our life. He is the whole
meaning of our life, the whole substance
of the monastic life. Nothing in the monastery makes sense if we forget this great
central truth.

But who is Jesus? He is the Son of
God, He is the Word who was made flesh
and dwelt among us. The monastic life,
like all Christian life, the life of the
Church, prolongs the mystery of the Incarnation on earth, and enables men to
receive into their souls, in great abun-
dance, the light and the charity of Christ.
We come to the monastery to live more

fully, more perfectly and more completely *in Christ*.

Therefore we can conclude that we come to the monastery to seek Christ — desiring that we may find Him and know Him, and thus come to live in Him and by Him.

And as we begin to find Him, we begin to realize at the same time that we have already been living in and by Him — for "He has first loved us."

II

The Word Was Made Flesh

The whole meaning of the monastic life flows from the mystery of the Incarnation. We come to the monastery, drawn by the action of the Holy Ghost, seeking eternal life. Eternal life is the life of God, given to us in Christ.

We come seeking truth. Christ said: "I am the truth." We come seeking life. He is also the way, and the life. We come seeking light. He is the "light of the world." We come seeking God. In Him "dwells all the fulness of the Godhead corporeally." (Col. 2:9.)

In Christ God has *revealed* Himself to us, and *given* Himself to us:

"The Word was made flesh and dwelt among us, and we saw His glory, the glory as it were of the only begotten Son of the Father, full of grace and truth." (John I:14.)

"By this has the charity of God appeared towards us, because He has sent His only begotten Son into the world, that we may live by Him." (I John 4:9.)

The question "Why have you come here?" is then the question Jesus asked in the Garden of the agony; *"Whom do you seek?"* We seek Jesus of Nazareth, Christ, the Son of the Living God, who descended from heaven for the love of us, who died for us on the Cross and rose from the dead and sits, alive, at the right hand of God the Father, filling us with His Life and directing us by His Spirit, so that He lives and breathes and works and acts and loves in us. Our purpose in life is then to grow in our union with the risen Christ, to live more and more deeply the life of His Body, the Church, to continue on earth the Incarnation which manifests the love of God for men, so that we may share in the glory of God with Christ in heaven.

The Word was made Flesh. *Verbum caro factum est.* This truth is the foundation stone of our monastic life. It is not just a truth which we know, and periodically meditate on. It is a truth which we must live by. Our whole life and all our activities must be steeped in the light which flows from it — that light is the radiance of God Himself. The Word is the Splendour of the Father's glory. He is the image of the invisible God and the exemplar of all God's creation. All things, all living beings, all inanimate creation, all spirits and intelligences, are created in Him, are sustained in Him, live in Him and by Him.

"In Him were all things created, in heaven and on earth, visible and invisible, whether thrones or dominations or principalities or powers: all things were created by Him and in Him. He is before all, and by Him all things consist." (Col. I:16-17.)

When St. Benedict saw all creation gathered together "as though in one ray of the sun" he saw all things in the light of the Word "without whom was made nothing that is made" and who "enlightens every man that comes into the world." (John 1: 3, 9.) This is the end to which we tend, to see the glory of the Word Incarnate, "the glory as of the only begotten of the Father, full of grace and truth." (John I:14.) We seek to see, and know, and love all things in Him — the world, the angels, our brothers; the Father and the Holy Spirit. This is the answer to the question, "Why did you come here, whom do you seek?"

He is All. And in order to see Him who is All, we must know and find ourselves in Him. We must find all things in Him. We must find the Father in Him.

The Word was made *flesh*. Incarnation! He took a human body and soul to Himself so that the Word dwelt among us as a Man. The Word did not assume flesh as a disguise, as a mere garment which could be cast off and thrown away. He became a Man. Jesus, a Man, is God. His Body is the Body of God. His Flesh is so full of the light and power of God that it is completely and totally divine.

And this Man-God, Jesus Christ, has become for us our new world, a new creation, in which all things are to be "recapitulated."

Dom Vonier says: "The Incarnation is adequately appreciated only by those to whom Christ's humanity is the marvel of marvels, a superb creation in which they have their being, in which they live, work, die, and in which they hope to rise again and in which they find the fulness of the Godhead as Moses found the fire in the bush." *(Complete Works of Abbot Vonier,* "The Christian Mind" — vol. I, p. 12.)

Jesus did not assume human nature only in order to die for us on the Cross and elevate us above "matter." The sacred Humanity of Christ reigning and active in heaven, is a *permanent principle* of sanctification, spiritualizing all that is brought in contact with Him by His Church.

If the Word was made flesh, and if the Body of Christ remains as a permanent source of sanctity, then bodily creation is not evil. God, when He created the world, "saw that it was good" (Gen. I) because it was made in Him and kept in existence by Him.

If our life is a search for Jesus, the Word made flesh, we must realize that we are not to act like pagan mystics, who repudiate the visible world as pure illu-

sion, and who seek to black out all contact with sensible and material things. On the contrary, we must begin by learning *how to see and respect the visible creation* which mirrors the glory and perfections of the invisible God.

Visible creation is held in being by the Word. But the Word Himself has entered into material creation to be its crown and its glory. The Divine King has entered into His own creation with a Body which is the summit of all created being. The Body of Christ is something greater and more wonderful than all the angelic creation, because it is hypostatically united to the Word, and St. Paul reminds us that we must prefer Him to all the angels.

"Beware lest any man cheat you by philosophy and vain deceit; according to the tradition of men, according to the elements of the world, and not according to Christ. For in Him dwells all the

fulness of the Godhead corporeally."
(Col. 2:8-9.)

If therefore we seek Jesus, the Word, we must be able to see Him in the created things around us — in the hills, the fields, the flowers, the birds and animals that He has created, in the sky and the trees. We must be able to see Him in nature. Nature is no obstacle to our contact with Him, if we know how to use it.

The Church uses material things in her Liturgy because she knows that they speak eloquently of God — she uses lights, incense, vestments, music. Above all she uses material things not only as symbols, but as means by which the grace of God is directly applied to our souls in the sacraments.

The Word, who was made Flesh, continues to make Himself present in His perfect Sacrifice, under the consecrated species of Bread and Wine.

If we are to live as Christians, as members of the Incarnate Word, we must remember that the life of our senses has also been elevated and sanctified by the grace of Christ — we must learn to use our senses to see and hear and appreciate the sacramental aids to holiness which the Church has given us. Hence the place of art, chant, and so on, as accessories to the Liturgy. We must be able to use our *imagination* in reading the Scriptures. We must respond to the living and inanimate beings which all declare the wisdom and glory of God their Creator.

We must, first of all, see all material things in the light of the mystery of the Incarnation. We must reverence all creation because the Word was made Flesh.

We can afford to reverence humble and material things, because the Church, the Body of Christ, remains in the midst of the world to sanctify it and shed upon all things the power of God's holy blessings. St. Paul says: "Every creature of God is good, and nothing is to be rejected that is accepted with thanksgiving. For it is sanctified by the word of God and prayer." (I Tim. 4:4-5.)

The monk, a man of prayer, must learn that through his prayers, through the blessing that is spread abroad by the presence of a monastery, the word is sanctified and brought close to God. He must rejoice in the fact that by his hidden union with Christ he enables all things to come closer to their last end, and to give glory to their Creator.

The monk must see the monastic community as Christ, living visible and present in the midst of His creation, and blessing all the surrounding country and all the things which the monks touch and use, leading all things to unite with us in praising God through His Incarnate Son. The material things which surround us are holy because of our bodies, which are sanctified by our souls, which are sanctified by the presence of the indwelling Word (cf. St. Bernard's sermons on the Dedication of a Church).

The created universe is a temple of God, in which our monastery is as it were the altar, the community in the tabernacle, and Jesus Himself is present in the Community, offering His homage of love and praise to the Father and sanctifying souls and all things.

Hence, in the monastic life, our senses are *educated* and elevated, rather than destroyed. But this education requires discipline. If our eyes are to be the eyes of the "new man" (Christ) they must no longer look upon things with the desires and prejudices of the "old man." They must be purified by faith, hope and love. While mortifying our senses, monastic asceticism gives them a new life in Christ, so that we learn to see, hear, feel,

taste, etc. as Christ, and even our senses
are then spiritualized.

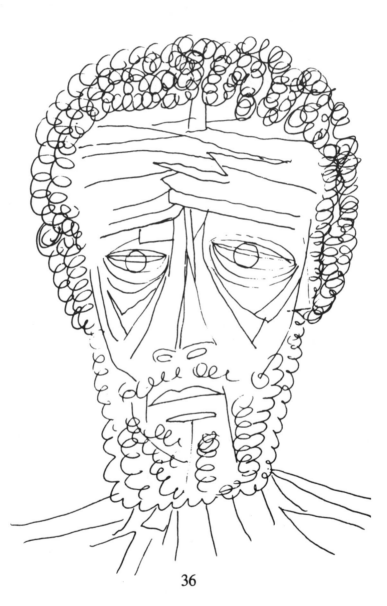

III

The Word of the Cross

All that we have said is only an introduction to the real mystery of our monastic vocation. God created the world, and saw that all things were good, for they subsisted in His Word. The Word was made flesh, and dwelt among us, and we saw the glory of God in Him. But is this all? If it is, then man has only to follow his natural instincts, make use of created things and he will easily and spontaneously find his way to God. But that is not the case. There are many obstacles to the "spiritualization" of our life. To become "new men" we have to struggle, fight, and even die.

We are fallen men, and the world has fallen with us. Man and the world were enslaved by the prince of darkness, and plunged into error and sin. Sin made it impossible for man to find his way back to God.

Although God's attributes are plainly visible in creation, man without God has, by his own fault, fallen into darkness and does not know God. "Although they knew God they did not glorify Him as God or give thanks, but became vain in their reasoning and their senseless minds were darkened, for while professing to be wise they have become fools." (Rom. I:21-22.)

Everywhere the New Testament puts us on our guard against the folly of a purely human kind of contemplation, and a purely human asceticism, which produce an illusion of holiness and wisdom, but cannot unite us with God or reconcile us with Him. Human ascetic and mystical techniques cannot save us from our sins. They keep us far from God, and take us even further from Him because their illusion engenders in us a false confidence and pride. They are centered on man, not on God; they tend to glorify man, not God.

St. Paul, in Romans, having pointed first to the pagan mysteries and other rites, then to the Law and the asceticism of the Jews, exclaims that neither of these can deliver man from sin and reconcile him to God. He quotes the words of the psalms we sing so often, in order to prove it:

> "Jews and Greeks are all under sin — There is not one just man, there is none who understands; there is none who seeks after God. All have gone astray together, they have become worthless. There is none who does good, no not even one.

Their throat is an open sepulchre; with their tongues they have dealt deceitfully. The venom of asps is beneath their lips; their mouth is full of cursing and bitterness. Their feet are swift to shed blood; destruction and misery are in their ways. And the path of peace they have not known. There is no fear of God before their eyes."

(Rom. 3:10 ff; cf. Psalms 13, 52, 5, 139, 35 and Isa. 59.)

St. Paul concludes: "All have sinned and all have need of the glory of God." (Rom. 3:23.)

The Old Testament tells us everywhere of a world that is displeasing to God, one which He is always on the point of destroying because of its wickedness.

"And God seeing that the wickedness of men was great on the earth and that all the thought of their heart was bent upon evil at all times, it repented Him that he had made man on the earth. And being touched inwardly with sorrow of heart, He said: I will destroy man whom I have created from the face of the earth, from man even to the beasts, from the creeping things even to the fowls of the air, for it repenteth me that I have made them." (Gen. 6:5-7.)

Such words as these give a tremendous urgency to our search for God, for Christ. We seek the Incarnate Word not only as the Creator and exemplar of all things, but far more as the *Redeemer,* the Savior of the world. The Word was made flesh in order to die on the Cross for the sins of mankind, and to reconcile fallen man to God.

The monk must always be conscious of the fact that without Christ there would be no salvation, no happiness, no joy, because man would be irrevocably cut off from God, the source of all life and joy. He must realize, above all, how utterly useless is human effort to please God, without Christ. Man cannot save himself, no matter how heroic may be his sacrifices, without Christ. But on the contrary once the sacrifice of the Cross is seen as our true salvation, then even the smallest act of charity becomes valuable and precious in the sight of God — even a cup of cold water.

The monk must be conscious of the infinite holiness of God, and of the offence which sin offers to that holiness. This consciousness of the holiness of God and of the offence of sin gives us the fear of the Lord which is the beginning of wisdom, and without which we cannot begin to pray as the Church would have us pray because we cannot have a true sense of spiritual realities. But we must

at the same time have an unbounded confidence in the Cross of Christ.

Here then is our situation — without Christ, we are entirely cut off from God, we have no access to Him, except in rites of natural religion which cannot save our souls of themselves (but we know that by the merits of the Passion of Christ God will give His grace to everyone who does what he can to live according to the light of his conscience). *With* and *in* Christ, all our lives are transformed and sanctified, and the smallest acts of love have their value as propitiation for sin.

We need a Savior in whom we will be born again to a new life, and ascend into heaven. God so loved the world that He has given us His Son to be our Savior. The more we appreciate this fact the greater our gratitude and trust, the more we will enter into the knowledge of God in Christ and serve Him with all hearts.

Jesus said — "No one has ascended into heaven except him who has descended from heaven, the Son of Man who is in heaven. And as Moses lifted up the serpent in the desert, even so must the Son of Man be lifted up, that those who believe in Him may not perish, but may have life everlasting." (John 3:13-14.)

All men need a Savior, and all have received Him in Christ who has died that all may be saved. "All are justified freely by His grace through the redemption of Christ Jesus." (Rom. 3:24.)

Whom, then, do we seek in the monastery? Not only God our Father and Creator — for even if we seek Him we cannot find Him without Christ. We seek Christ our Savior and Redeemer, in whom we are reconciled to the Father. Or rather, we seek the Father in Him; for as St. Paul says: "God was truly in Christ reconciling the world to Himself;" and "Christ died for all in order that all who are alive may live no longer for themselves but for Him who died for them and rose again." (2 Cor. 5:19, 15.)

"We seek Christ Crucified as our redemption, as our strength, our wisdom, our life in God." (I Cor. I:23-24.)

We cannot fully understand this if we do not understand the love and compassion of Christ for us in our weakness. It was the Pelagians who saw the Cross only as a challenge and an inspiration, not as a power, a source of life and strength. Christ is not just a sublime hero whom we must strive with every nerve to imitate — He is a loving Savior who has come down to our level to give us His strength. He willed to identify Himself and our weakness in Gethsemani and on the Cross.

We seek Jesus not only as our personal, individual salvation, but as the salvation and the unity of all mankind. The original solidarity of man, on which our perfect happiness and fulfilment depend, was destroyed by sin and man cannot find peace and unity within himself, or in society, until he is reconciled to God in Christ. Christ is our peace, with one another, with ourselves, and with God. Therefore we seek Him as the Savior of the world, as the Prince of Peace, who will restore the unity of mankind in His Kingdom of Peace.

The Redemption which Jesus came to bring, was offered to all by His death on the Cross: we receive our Redemption by mystically dying together with Him and rising with Him from the dead, "since one died for all, therefore all died." (2 Cor. 5:14.)

The monk who prays in the fear of God and thanks God for the infinite love with which He has sent His son to redeem us, realizes not only that Jesus died for him individually, but that He died for the Church. That He loved the Church and came to unite all mankind to God in a unity of Spirit to the Father in Himself, "Christ also loved the Church and delivered Himself up for her, that He might sanctify her in a bath of water by means of the word." (Eph. 5:25.)

This is the "word of the Cross" (or the doctrine of the Cross) which is "foolishness to those who perish, but to those who are saved, that is to us, it is the power of God." (I Cor. 1:17.)

This doctrine is the heart of our whole life of prayer and penance.

If we understand these things, we will understand the Divine Office, and see what we are praying for. In the Psalms we are constantly contemplating, in mystery, the great reality of our Redemption in Christ. We are thanking God for that Redemption, we are pleading for the whole Church, and for those who do not know God. We are begging God to forgive sin, and to save those who are immersed in the darkness of sin. We are begging that we may all come to the vision of His glory, and that His Christ may be glorified in us.

More than that, we come to realize that it is Jesus Himself, praying in us, who continues, in our Divine Office, His work of redeeming the world. The monk is united with Jesus as a Savior, in the Office, and above all in the Mass.

IV

Children of the Resurrection

Christ having died on the Cross and risen from the dead, "dieth now no more." He sits at the right hand of the Father, and has become for us a "life-giving spirit." (I Cor. 15:45.)

Just as Adam, when he came from the hand of the Creator, was to be the head of the human race and the principle of natural life, so Christ when He entered into His glory by the Resurrection, became the Head of a new mankind, joined to Him in one Mystical Body, and vivified by contact with His Sacred Humanity which had now become "life-giving spirit." That is to say that the Humanity of the Word reigning in heaven as the

"Christ" or the "Anointed" of the Father sends into our souls and bodies the Divine Spirit.

Our monastic life does not consist merely in having Jesus for a Savior whom we thank and adore, while He reigns in heaven or in the tabernacle — it is a life which is nourished by constant spiritual contact with the Glorified Humanity of Christ the Savior, who lives in us by His grace and is thus the principle of our supernatural life — "life-giving spirit."

Our point of contact with the Risen Savior is faith in His Cross. By faith we submit our minds and hearts entirely to Him and to the power of the divine life of charity. Charity then becomes the principle of a new activity, of the good works by which we serve the Living God — we are then "cleansed from *dead works*" — the things we do have a totally new and spiritual character in Christ. They give glory to God, they build up the

Body of Christ, they merit for us an increase in our union with Him who is our holiness.

Contact with the Risen Humanity of Christ is true holiness. Growth in holiness is growth in our union with the Risen Christ. But Christ lives and acts in His Church. Growth in union with the Church, deeper participation in the prayer life of the Church, in her sacramental life, in her other activities, gives us a deeper sharing in the life and mind and prayer of Christ Himself. The life of a monk is immersed in the depths of the Church's life in Christ. The monk is essentially a *vir ecclesiae,* a man of the Church.

Our spiritual life is the life of the Spirit of Christ in His Church. It is the life that flows from contact with Christ as "life-giving spirit." To have a truly spiritual life is then to think and love and act not just as Christ *would* act in a given situation, but as He precisely *does* act, by His grace, in us, at the moment. It is to live and act with the mind of the Church, which is the mind of Christ.

In other words, our life in Christ is something more than imitation from afar, a moral reproduction in our lives, of a pattern offered by Jesus in the Gospels. We do not simply open a "Life of Christ," and then by our own power and ingenuity and good will put into effect, humanly, the things which we read. Such efforts are necessary, but unless they are on an entirely supernatural plane they have little fruit for our spirit.

Our life in Christ, our actions in Christ, are those in which Christ, living within us by grace, inspires our thoughts and acts by the movements of His Holy Spirit of love springing up from within the depths of our own souls.

Speaking of this spiritual life as divine wisdom, St. Paul points out that we cannot know the things of God unless we receive the Spirit of God, who gives us a deep insight into the hidden secrets of the mind and will of God. (I Cor. 2:9-12.) To be thus taught and moved by the Holy Spirit is to have the "mind of Christ." (I Cor. 2:16.)

But the wisdom of the Spirit, which gives us the "mind of Christ," is entirely opposed to another wisdom, the wisdom of the "flesh" and of the "sensual man who does not perceive the things that are of the Spirit of God for it is foolishness to him and he cannot understand because it is examined spiritually." (I Cor. 2:14.)

Jesus insisted that we had to be born again to the life of the spirit precisely because: "It is the spirit that gives life, the flesh profits nothing." (John 6:64.) "That which is born of the flesh is flesh, and that which is born of the spirit is spirit." (John 3:6.) And Saint Paul adds: "What a man sows that he will also reap.

For he that sows in the flesh from the flesh shall also reap corruption. But he who sows in the spirit from the spirit will reap life everlasting." (Gal. 5:8.)

We are caught in a bitter conflict between the flesh and the spirit. Jesus has delivered us from sin, but not from the weaknesses and concupiscences of the flesh. We have to reproduce in our life the Cross of Christ so that, having died sacramentally to sin in baptism and penance, we may also put to death sin in our flesh by restraining our evil desires and bad tendencies. This is the basis for our life of monastic asceticism.

Hence our whole monastic life implies an obligation to discipline ourselves and renounce ourselves in order to live in and by the Spirit of Christ. The ascetic life is both negative and positive, and the positive element of Christian asceticism is the more important. St. Paul sums up

the whole meaning of Christian asceticism with such phrases as these:

> "Walk in the Spirit and you will
> not fulfil the lusts of the flesh."
> (Gal. 5:16.)

You see that he first says "Walk in the Spirit" — the positive side of asceticism — and the negative part follows as a logical consequence, as an immediate effect, "you will not fulfil the lusts of the flesh."

> "They who belong to Christ
> have crucified their flesh with its
> passions and desires. If we live
> by the Spirit, by the Spirit let us
> also walk." (Gal. 5:24-25.)
> "Therefore, brethren, we are
> debtors not to the flesh, that we
> should live according to the
> flesh, for if you live according
> to the flesh you will die, but if
> by the spirit you put to death the

deeds of the flesh you shall live." (Rom. 8:12.)

Note the expression "*debtors* to the flesh." The flesh is like a usurer — who gives a little in order to take everything — constantly strengthening his hold on the one in his power, and exacting a more and more servile submission.

Let us consider what St. Paul means by the works of the flesh. When the Bible speaks of flesh and spirit, it does not mean to oppose the material element in man to his spiritual element, as if the body were evil and only the soul were good. On the contrary, both terms refer to the whole man, body and soul. The whole man is "flesh" if his body and his selfish passions dominate his soul. The whole man is "spirit" if his soul is subject to the Spirit of Christ and his body is subject to the soul. To live "in the Spirit" therefore does not mean living without a body. It means suffering temptations and trial. It means labor, and all the normal conditions of man's life on earth.

"The inclination of the flesh, which is death" (Rom. 8:5) leads us to all kinds of sin. Not only to sins of sensuality and carnal lust, but also to sins against religion — like witchcraft, magic, superstition, idolatry, and especially to sins against charity, sins which divide us against our brother, like envy, enmities, jealousies, contentions, factions, parties, anger, and even murder. (See Gal. 5:19-21.) The works of the flesh which are most stressed by St. Paul are those which divide the Body of Christ into factions.

"Since there are jealousy and strife among you, are you not carnal and walking as mere men?" (I Cor. 3:3.)

"If you have bitter jealousy and contentions in your hearts, do not glory and be liars against the truth. This is not the wisdom that descends from above, it is earthly, sensual, devilish." (James 3:14-15.)

The Pharisees were ascetics, yet theirs were "dead works," they lived "in the flesh" and were enemies of the Cross of Christ.

The action of the Holy Spirit in our lives produces joy and peace, unity with our brethren, and in order to do this the Spirit teaches us obedience and humility. This explains the great importance of these fundamental virtues in the Rule of St. Benedict. In studying and keeping the Holy Rule we must realize the function of these virtues is not only to gain merit for our souls and to exercise us in self-discipline, but also and above all *to unite us with Christ in His Body the Church.* They are virtues without which we cannot begin to keep His commandment that we "abide in Him."

The Benedictine ascesis of silence, obedience, solitude, humility, manual labor, liturgical prayer, is all designed to unite us with the Mystical Christ, with one another in charity, and its aim to bring our souls under the complete dominance of the Holy Spirit. The Benedictine way of humility in the common life is precisely the best way to help us "walk in the Spirit." St. Benedict himself indicates this (end of ch. 7).*

If we follow our monastic Lawgiver, we will taste the fruit of the Spirit which is: "charity, joy, peace, patience, kindness, goodness, faith, modesty, continency." (Gal. 5:22.)

St. Benedict in his Rule makes it quite clear that the whole aim of the Benedictine life is to form Christ in us, to enable the Spirit of Christ to carry out, in our lives, actions worthy of Christ. We reproduce His obedience and humility when, like Him, we can truly say: "I did

*The Holy Rule of St. Benedict. In Chapter 7, St. Benedict defines 12 degrees of humility for which a monk should strive.

not come to do my own will, but the will of Him who sent me." (2nd degree of humility.) We reproduce His Passion when, like Him, we are made "obedient unto death" (3rd degree of humility), when we suffer all things patiently and perseveringly for love of Him (4th degree of humility) and when we are, like our divine Savior, reduced to nothing, a "worm and no man" (7th degree of humility). Having ascended all the degrees of humility, our hearts are empty of self, and God Himself can produce the likeness of Christ in us by the action of His Spirit, who brings joy and consolation in all the aspects of the monastic life: *delectatio virtutum quae Dominus jam in operario suo mundo a vitiis et peccatis, Spiritu Sancto dignabitur demonstrare* (Rule, c. 7). ["...a delight in virtue which God will vouchsafe to manifest by the Holy Spirit in his laborer, now cleansed from vice and sin."]

V

Sons and Heirs of God

The positive side of monastic asceticism is always more important than the negative.

What matters most is not so much what we deny ourselves and give up (the flesh), but the new life which develops in us in proportion as we are emptied of self (the life of the Holy Spirit). In any case, we could not carry on the work of emptying ourselves and purifying ourselves unless the Spirit of God helped our weakness. (Rom. 8:29.)

When we arrive at the purity of heart which is the fruit of monastic asceticism, of humility and obedience, then the Spirit of God, who has gained possession of our hearts, "gives testimony to our spirit that we are the sons of God." (Rom. 8:16.) Not only that, but we receive a conviction of the truth that we have entered with Christ, in mystery, into all the good things of God. We are heirs of God and joint-heirs with Christ. (Rom. 8:17.) We are sons of God because we are led by the Spirit of God. (Rom. 8:14.) And to be led by the Holy Spirit is to live in joy, confidence, exultation and interior liberty, for the spirit of divine sonship is a spirit of freedom. It is not, and cannot be, a spirit of bondage and fear. The spirit of freedom is the spirit of the heavenly Jerusalem, the Church. It is the freedom with which Christ has made us free. (Gal. 4:21-31.)

We have a holy obligation to defend this freedom and joy, and to live always in the Spirit, not allowing ourselves to be caught "under the yoke of slavery" (Gal. 5:1) to the "elements of this world." (Col. 2:8.) We must not allow ourselves to be enslaved by the flesh in any form — whether sensuality, or license, or self-love, or disobedience, or purely human forms of religious observance — for example, the formalism and vain observance which accompany self-will and pride in our religious life.

If we are sons of God, then the Spirit of God prays in us, and St. Paul says this is necessary, for by ourselves "we do not know what we should pray for as we ought." (Rom. 8:26.)

The prayer of the Holy Spirit in His Church, the prayer that is always sure of reaching the very depths of the Heart of God and giving Him infinite glory, is the *Liturgy*. In the Liturgy, Christ Himself is present as High Priest in the midst of His Holy People. The prayer of the Church is the prayer of Christ. It is the prayer of salvation, sanctification, and redemption.

Pius XII says that in the Liturgy "Through His Spirit in us, Christ entreats the Father" *(Mediator Dei)*. He adds: "In assuming human nature, the Divine Word introduced into this earthly exile a hymn which is sung in heaven for all eternity. He unites to Himself the whole human race and with it sings this hymn of praise to God" *(Mediator Dei)*. At every liturgical function, Jesus the Head of the Church is present with His whole Mystical Body, offering praise to the Father and sanctifying the souls of men.

Therefore it is clear that in the Liturgy we find Jesus as our Redeemer and Sanctifier. But it is above all in the Mass, which is the very heart of the Liturgy, that we discover Christ Himself, and ourselves in Him.

The Mass, particularly the Conventual Mass, is the very heart of the monastic life because in it the monastic community and all the persons who go to make it up, unite with Christ the High Priest in the very Mystery of His great Redemptive act which is made present upon the altar. At every Mass Christ is present to us as immolated and risen from the dead, and the Church is immolated and rises with Him. At every Mass, the new life of the Spirit, the life of the sons of God, is renewed in us as we participate in the sacrifice of the Divine High Priest, the Lamb of God who takes away the sins of the world.

The Mass is the very heart of our monastic sacrifice of ourselves to God. At every Mass and Communion we *live* the very essence of our monastic immolation of ourselves with Christ. At the Consecration we bow down and *renew our total surrender to the will of God* in and with Jesus Crucified. At Mass we enter into the holy of holies, the sanctuary of heaven, with Him. At Mass, the whole Body of Christ stands before the face of the Heavenly Father and adores

His infinite holiness, makes perfect repa-
ration for all sin, thanks Him for all His
gifts and above all thanks Him for His
great glory *(gratias agimus tibi propter
magnam gloriam tuam)*. In so doing, the
Church also petitions Him for mercy and
for grace and for all the temporal blessings that we need in order to live as sons
of God. Above all, in Communion we are
sacramentally united to the risen and
glorified Savior, the principle of our life
"in the Spirit." We are also united to one
another more closely in the Spirit of
Christ, because by our Communion we
grow in charity.

It is in the Mass and the Liturgy that
we are most truly and perfectly monks,
because it is there that we most fully live
our life in Christ, finding Him whom we
have come to seek, submitting in and with
Him to the Father's will.

Now our *manual labor* gives practical
expression to our obedience. We see

every assignment as the will of God. We put aside our own tastes, our own will and our own opinions and hasten to do the work assigned to us as Jesus Himself hastened to do the will of the Father. We say with Him: "my meat is to do the will of Him that sent me."

Also in manual labor we become helpers and co-operators with God the Creator and administrator of the world — we become instruments of His Divine Providence — we help Him change and renew the face of the earth. We are agents and tools of the Creator Spirit. Like Adam, we are privileged to be the gardeners of God's creation, and to contemplate God in and through the creatures we work with.

Finally, by our manual labor we help to feed and clothe ourselves and our brethren and we also contribute to the support of the poor. We are thus not only carrying out the Father's will, in obedience, but in charity we are feeding and clothing Christ who comes to us hungry and naked and poor.

In order to live the Liturgy, we must give ourselves to *Lectio Divina* (Spiritual Reading). Here, too, we seek and find Christ. Here as in the Liturgy we find Him in His word. "For the word of God is living and efficient and keener than any two-edged sword, and extending even to the division of the soul and spirit, of joints also and of marrow, and a discerner of the thoughts and intentions of the heart." (Heb. 4:12.) In our search for God, we quickly come to realize that He is found in His words, for they alone, before the Incarnation of the Word Himself, could bridge the abyss that separates us from His infinite holiness. The word of God is filled with His infinite creative power: He spoke, and all things were made. His word has power to save our souls: we must purify our hearts in order

to "receive the ingrafted word that is able to save your souls." (James I:22.)

Hence the need of monastic silence, in order that the monk may be "swift to hear and slow to speak." (James I:19.) God spoke His eternal Word in silence, and He wishes us to receive His words in silence. If we are merely speculative students of Scripture, breaking the words of God up into scientific fragments and deafening our spirit with the noise of human argument — which is too often the noise of the "flesh" with its spirit of factions and divisions — then we cannot hear the Word who speaks to us silently in the words of God.

The monk will always remember that "he who is of God hears the words of God" (John 8:47.) and he is always attuned to the coming of God in His words, since each morning he sings in the invitatory of Vigils (Ps. 94): *Hodie si vocem ejus audieritis nolite obdurare corda ves-*

tra! "Today if you should hear His voice, harden not your hearts."

What does the Holy Spirit say to us in our reading of Scripture? He teaches us to see in Scripture the great themes which we have been treating as fundamental in the monastic life — the Word made Flesh, the Divine Redeemer uniting to Himself a "perfect people" living in Him, by His Spirit, and united through Him to the Father. More particularly the Holy Spirit enlightens us, in our reading, to see how *our own lives* are part of these great mysteries — how we are one with Jesus in them. And then the Holy Spirit opens our eyes and attunes our hearts to the future, the consummation of all and the glory of Christ in His Church.

Both in his spiritual reading and in his liturgical praise, the monk prays as an individual and as a member of Christ, listens to God as a person and as a member of the Church. Liturgy demands of us the sacrifice of what is merely individualistic and eccentric in our lives, that we may rise above ourselves to the supra-personal level of the Spouse of Christ. In the Liturgy we must sacrifice and lose something of ourselves in order to find ourselves again on a higher level. But the Liturgy can never make us mere automatons praising God like machines. On the contrary, liturgical praise is the *collective interior prayer* of persons who are fully conscious of themselves as members of Christ. There is and can be no contradiction between Liturgy and personal prayer. If our liturgical prayer is not also *personal* and *interior,* if it does not spring spontaneously from our own freedom and our own interior spirit, from the inviolable sanctuary of our own deepest will, then it is not a prayer at all. In order that our liturgical prayer may always have this interior and personal quality, we must frequently enter into the inner chamber of our own heart outside the time of choral prayer, and pray to the Father in secret. This is necessary if we are to keep alive the spontaneity and freedom which are the most precious contribution we can bring to the Liturgy, and without which our liturgical prayer will be a "dead work."

Liturgy, spiritual reading, and private contemplative prayer all work together to deepen our life in Christ, and all have an absolute importance which cannot be replaced. No one of them, by itself, can satisfy all the interior needs and aspirations of the monk's soul. No one of them must ever be allowed to crowd out the others. In all of them the monk seeks and finds Christ, but if he seeks Christ in Liturgy alone, then the Liturgy will become formalism. If he seeks Him in private contemplation alone, then his contemplative prayer will become illuminism — or will degenerate into daydreaming or even sleep. If he seeks Him in work alone, he will fall into the sin of activism.

In short, all the monk's prayer life is and must be a life of *prayer in the Spirit.* The Spirit of Christ, while praying in us in the Liturgy, "reminds us of everything Jesus has said." The same Spirit who drove Jesus into the desert that He might be tempted by the devil, leads us into the wasteland of interior trial in which our love is tested and purified. Finally, the spirit of Sonship enables us to experience our union with the Father in the Son, crying out within us "Abba, Father." Our prayer life is mature when, in our prayer, the Spirit of God, having purified our love and made us obedient and humble, raises us up to God our Father in a spirit of liberty and confidence, because the *experience of His mercy* makes us sure that we are His Sons. (Read Rom. 5:1-5.)

The whole ascetic life of the monk, in all its aspects both positive and negative, is summed up in his consecration of himself, his whole life, all that he has and all that he is, to God, by his five monastic vows. The life of the monk is the life of the vows. One of the most important of these vows is that of conversion of manners *(conversatio morum),* which is not properly understood if we regard it merely as a special vow to "tend to perfection." Conversion of manners means striving to change one's whole life and all one's attitudes from those of the world to those of the cloister. By conversion of manners we definitely consecrate our whole life to the service of God as monks, men who have turned their backs on the world, who have substituted the humility, chastity, poverty, renunciation of the cloister for the ambitions, comforts, pleasures, riches and self-satisfaction of the world. Obedience means the renunciation of our own will, in order to carry out in our whole life the will of another who represents God. Stability means renouncing our freedom to travel about from place to place, and binds us to one monastery until death. Poverty and Chastity are not explicitly mentioned in the Rule of St. Benedict because they were considered by him to be included in conversion of manners, but they form an essential part of the monk's obligations.

VI

Spouse of Christ

The monastic life of humility, obedience, liturgical prayer, spiritual reading, penance, manual labour, contemplation, tends to ever purify the soul of the monk and lead him to intimacy with Christ in that sacred virginity which makes him worthy of marriage with the Word of God. This spirit of virginity is the true essence of the contemplative life which is our vocation.

We are not contemplatives by the mere fact of living an enclosed and penitential life. We can indeed be more active, more restless and more distracted in the cloister than we would be in the active life, if we do not possess the interior virginity of spirit, the silence and peace of soul, which enable us to find God in His word, to listen to the words of Christ, to move with the breathings of the Holy Spirit within us.

The virginity of spirit to which we are called is a purity of heart in which our souls preserve their baptismal innocence, or the innocence of the second baptism of our vows, and offer themselves in perfect purity to God. Virginity of soul does not preclude temptations and trials, but the deep spirit of faith which it implies enables us always to rise above the flesh and its storms in order to meditate on the incorruptible beauty of the Word. St. Augustine defines virginity as: *in carne corruptibili incorruptionis perpetua meditatio.* * The life of the virgin soul that is the spouse of Christ is a life lived in the pure, limpid radiance of the Word Himself.

*"In corrutible flesh, perpetual meditation of what is incorruptible."

Spiritual virginity is not arrived at by violence or strain. The first step is the total acceptance of our self, our whole being, as God has willed us to be — the acceptance of all the parts of our being — body and soul, mind and instinct, emotions and will, in order to give all to God in the harmony of a balanced and spiritualized personality.

The purpose of our monastic vows is to stabilize us in a life of union to the will of God, to keep us unceasingly united to His will in all things until death. The vows therefore protect us in our striving for virginity of spirit. They are one of the great means to that virginity. Chastity preserves us from being tainted by the flesh. Poverty keeps our soul unspoiled by the desire of material possessions or by anxiety about ourselves. Stability makes us renounce the urge to travel and to change our way of life. Obedience protects us from the corruption of self-will. Conversion of manners aims directly at spiritual virginity — by orienting our whole life to God in faith and love — The vow of *conversatio morum* is a vow to live "in the Spirit."

The virginity of spirit which keeps us united to the Word is the perfection of the monastic life. By it, the monk not only renounces human marriage, but rather lays hands upon the supernatural and mystical reality of which marriage is only an external symbol — the union of love which joins the soul to God "in one spirit." Virginity of spirit keeps the soul in constant contact with the Holy Word of God, the sanctity of God Himself. Above all, sacred virginity makes visible the union of the Church with Christ her Divine Spouse. Pope Pius XII says:

> "The most delicate fruit of virginity is this, that virgins make tangible as it were the perfect virginity of their Mother the Church and the sanctity of her

intimate union with Christ...The greatest glory of the virgins is undoubtedly to be the living images of the perfect integrity of the union of the Church and her divine Spouse." *(Sacra Virginitas.)*

This is the end and the perfection of the monastic vocation: to find Christ, the Word, to cling to Him in the purity of perfect love and unalterable peace, and to say with the Bride in the Canticles: "I found Him whom my soul loveth: I held Him: and I will not let Him go." (Cant. 3:4.) From this it is clear that the whole monastic life is lived in and with Mary the Virgin Mother who has given us the Word incarnate. She is the model and the summary of all monastic spirituality, and the Fathers could call her the "rule of monks" — *Maria regula monachorum.*

A life "in the Spirit" is then a life of spiritual virginity, in which we are moved not by our own desires, tastes, aptitudes, feelings and nature, but by the will and love of God. In such a life, we are completely conformed to the Virgin Mother of God, who by the perfect simplicity of her faith received into her Immaculate Heart the full light of the Word and, having clothed Him in her virginal flesh, by the action of the Holy Spirit, gave Him to be the Savior of the world.

Hence to live "in the Spirit" is in effect to live in and by Mary, the Bride of the Holy Spirit. Life in the Spirit is a life which she herself has obtained for us and given to us as Mediatrix of all grace. The movements of our life in the Spirit are directed by her Motherly Heart. To acknowledge Mary perfectly as our Queen is then to abandon ourselves entirely to the action of the Holy Spirit, who comes to us through her.

If Mary becomes our Queen and our "Rule," the inspirations of the Holy

Spirit will tend more and more to reproduce in our lives the virginal detachment and the pure love of God which led Mary to submit her whole being entirely to the will of God. We will be led by the Holy Spirit to make our religious consecration a true replica of Mary's *fiat*. We will not only give ourselves to God in one way or another but we will give ourselves *as she did.*

Spiritual virginity therefore implies an emptiness of self, a forgetfulness of self, which can only exist in so far as we renounce all deliberate complacency in anything that is not willed by God — and when doing His will, rest not in the thing we do but in Him for whom we do it.

In this way, we see that spiritual virginity is impossible as long as we remain concerned with ourselves, our plans, our ideas, or even with our ideals — *a fortiori* with persons and objects for their own sakes.

Many souls in religion do good things and lead lives that are more or less virtuous, they avoid faults and strive for perfection, but in all that they do they are motivated more by their own desires and their own will than by the will of God. They think of Him of course, but unconsciously they keep Him in the background. Rather than being *moved by* His will, they do what they think fit and then offer it to Him for His approval. They do not think first and foremost — "What does God want of me?" but rather "What do I want?" and then they dutifully ask "Does God permit it? Will He accept it?" Their life is a conscientious effort to do what they want to do, in such a way as to avoid offending God. But this is not virginity of spirit. The virgin spirit is not "married" to its own will or its own plans. It is free — unattached. It is available. It is expendable. God can come at any moment and find the will empty and free, waiting for His initiative. That is all that matters!

Spiritual virginity is not merely *emptiness* or *absence* of other beings. Here again, the positive aspect of virginity is the more important. Virginity does not consist merely in being free and detached from creatures, but in being *united to God,* as we sing in the Office of St. Agnes: *"Quem cum amavero munda sum, cum tetigero casta sum, cum accepero, virgo sum. "* (Whom when I have loved I am pure, when I have touched I am chaste, when I have accepted I am a virgin).

The perfection of spiritual virginity is then the mystical marriage of the soul with the Word. Of this marriage, St. Bernard says:

> "The soul that loves God perfectly is married to Him. What is more delectable than this likeness between the soul and God?

What is more to be desired than that charity which brings it about that, not content with the teaching of human masters, thou approachest, O soul, the Word Himself, and remaineth constantly united to Him, familiarly turning to Him in everything, consulting Him about all that goes on: thy intellect is as capable of knowing Him, now, as thy will is courageous in its desires....This is no mere contract between the soul and the Word, it is a perfect union in which the fact of willing and not-willing the same things makes one spirit out of two beings." (Sermo 83 *In Cantica.*)

In order to be perfectly what God wants us to be we must be truly ourselves. But in order to be truly ourselves we must find ourselves in Christ —

which can only be done if we lose our-selves in Him. This is our great vocation.

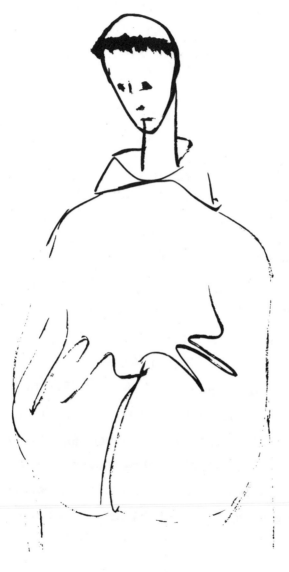

Conclusion

The monastic life is a *search for God* and
not a mission to accomplish this or that
work for souls. The monk fulfils his
function in the Church in proportion as
he finds God in the peculiar way that God
makes possible for Him. Each of us will
find God in his own way, but all of us
together will find Him by living together
in the Spirit, in perfect charity, as members of one another in Christ, recognizing
the fact that Christ lives in us both as a
community and as individuals. Our vocation is to live by the will of God in prayer
and sacrifice that we may become able to
see and glorify Christ in His Church and
reach perfect union with Him by the
action of the Spirit, in the sanctuary of

our own souls. Thus we return, through Christ, to the Father of all.

We must never forget that we will not be able to do this unless we have really renounced the past and left the world for the love of God. It is not possible to be a monk and at the same time to live in the monastery in a spirit of compromise, retaining all the comforts and ambitions and concerns that characterize life in the world. Without a true *metanoia,* a true conversion of one's whole life, monastic discipline is an illusion. There must be a total reorientation of our entire being from the love of self to the love of God. The monk cultivates "contempt" for the world in the sense in which the world is opposed to God. But at the same time he retains his love for and concern with all those souls redeemed by Christ, who are struggling to find Him and serve Him even in the midst of the world — and above all for those who, loved and sought

by Christ, never think of Him and have never, perhaps, heard His Holy Name.

EPILOGUE:
The Monk in
a Changing World

It would be an illusion to think that the monk could live entirely unrelated to the rest of the world. As an individual, it is true, he retains only a minimum of contact with worldly society. He lives in solitude, far from the cities of men. He does not go out to preach or teach. He remains in the cloister contemplating and praising God. Nevertheless, he is inextricably involved in the common sufferings and problems of the society in which he lives. From these sufferings and problems there is and can be no escape. On the contrary, they may perhaps be felt more acutely, because in a more spiritual form, in the cloister. Far from being exempted from service in the battles of his age, the monk, as a Soldier of Christ, is appointed to fight these battles on a spiritual, hidden front — in mystery — by prayer and self-sacrifice. He cannot do this unless he is somehow in contact with the rest of the world, somehow identified with the others who suffer outside the cloister walls and for whom he is fighting in his solitude, fighting not against flesh and blood "but against principalities and powers, against the rulers of the world of this darkness, and against the spirits of wickedness in the high places." (Eph. 6:12.)

Hence, though the monk is withdrawn from the world, he preserves an intimate spiritual contact with those with whom he is actually or potentially united "in Christ" — in the Mystery of our unity in the Risen Savior, the Son of God. He feels that he has them all in his heart and that they are in him and with him as he stands before the throne of God. Their needs are his own, their interests are his interests, their joys and sorrows are his, for he has identified himself with them not only by a realization that they all share one human nature, but above all by the charity of Christ, poured forth in our hearts by the Holy Spirit who is given to us in Christ.

And so the monk must have some general idea of the world in which he lives. He will not profit by losing himself in the maze of political entanglements which is only on the surface of history. He will perhaps understand the history of his age better if he knows less of what takes up space on the front pages of the newspapers. He will have a different, and perhaps more accurate, perspective.

He must realize clearly that the world of the twentieth century is in a state of crisis because it is going through a change more sudden and more profound than anything that has ever happened before. It is a complete upheaval of the whole human race, and no one can say with assurance what will be the final result of this transformation. One thing only is certain, the world as we know it, society as we know it, will be even more radically changed in the next fifty years than they have been in the first half of the century. And this means that by the end of the twentieth century our society will be unrecognizable, by the standards of the nineteenth century and of the ages which preceded it.

In this changing world the Church, against which the gates of hell shall not prevail, has a permanent place. The monk, an integral part of the Mystical Christ, also has his permanent place in the changing world of man. And this means that in some respects the Church and the monastic order have to change, since they cannot keep in touch with the rest of men otherwise. The changes will be superficial and accidental, external, secondary. The deep hidden essence of the Christian and monastic life will remain what it always has been. But secondary attitudes, customs, observances, and practices, have always changed with the times and will do so again.

The monk in our world is then faced with a responsibility towards God, towards himself, and towards the rest of the world. He must see to it that his monastic life is firmly rooted in the essential truths of Christianity, that he lives in the Mystery of Christ. Otherwise, if his monastic life and ideal consists in what is secondary and accidental, all will vanish in the process of change. For — we repeat — it is certain that the changes through which our world must pass will require the sacrifice of many secondary and transient aspects of the Christian and monastic lives. The essentials will emerge necessarily in all the greater clarity and strength after this transformation.

As examples of what is "accidental" and "secondary" in the monastic life, we may include everything which is proper only to a particular age or nation or culture — for instance, the custom of using Gothic architecture for monastic buildings, or certain special forms of religious habit or certain fashions in piety, such as devotion to a particular saint or attachment to some devout practices which are not universal. Also the outlook and spirituality of monks may vary, in accidentals, from age to age.

But in its essentials — solitude, poverty, obedience, silence, humility, manual labor, prayer and contemplation — monastic spirituality does not change.

The transformation through which the world must pass will not be merely political. It is indeed an illusion to think that the forces which are at work in our modern society are, above all, political. The great political movements of our time, so complex and so often apparently so meaningless, are the smoke screen behind which are developing the evolutions of a spiritual war too great for men to wage by any human plan. This is something that is going on in the whole of mankind, and it would go on even if there were no political movements. The politicians are only the instruments of force which they themselves ignore. These forces are more powerful and more spiritual than man.

Behind and beyond the action of created forces, whether human or superhuman, we know that the Supreme Wisdom of God is working inexorably, through all these agents in combat with one another, for a solution that transcends the particularized interests of various groups and sections of mankind. The monk, hidden in the Mystery of Christ, should be, of all men, the one most aware of this hidden action of the divine Will. This he will surely be if he is a man of sacrifice, pure in heart, a man of prayer.

This brings us face to face with the great problem of Communism. And the problem must not be oversimplified. It must be confronted in its reality and its complexity, without wishful thinking, and without the benefit of magical incantations.

Three things about Communism: First of all, its techniques are tremendously effectively in one respect. The machinery of Communism is geared for one job and one only: *the seizure of power*. The abstract ideals to which Communism subscribes are not fixed *a priori* ideals which must be realized at all costs. Communism is essentially opportunistic and pragmatic. It diagnoses the weaknesses of society, and takes full advantage of them to destroy the existing order of things and substitute for it a Red dictatorship. The ideology is so flexible that it can change completely overnight, and does repeatedly change to fit each new set of circumstances. Hence, it is right to say that in Communism the ideology is only a façade. It has no real meaning in itself. The Reds have the gift of being able to make themselves believe anything they like. Communism assumes that once the Reds have power the future can be left to take care of itself. It will, indeed! But not in the optimistic sense in which they expect it to.

The democracies, on the other hand, are committed to certain ideals by their very nature. We are bound to act on an *a priori* belief in liberty, truth, justice, the dignity of the individual, equal opportunities for all, etc. This is not the place to discuss the question whether these values actually flourish among us as we say they do. The point is, as long as we believe in such things, we are prevented from using the effective totalitarian techniques

which in practice cast them all aside in order to seize power.

We cannot make a ruthless, indiscriminate use of lies, violence, and unjust coercion in order to attain our ends. Hence, the paradox that our very ideals are a handicap in the battle to defend our ideal of liberty. The danger is that we may finally renounce our ideals in practice in order to fight Communism with its own ruthlessness. In that case, we will be falling into the same totalitarian error, and will defeat ourselves.

The second fact about Communism: it has a tremendous hold over those who have actually committed themselves to it. There are millions who really believe in Communism, who are united behind their leaders, corrupt though they may be, and are filled with the conviction that they are absolutely right and that everyone else is in illusion. Admittedly, this unshaken conviction is so irrational as to savor of paranoia — but that only makes it all the more dangerous. The relative sanity which still prevails in the free world brings with it the laudable weakness of hesitation and disagreement. No one man, no one group or nation, is so entirely convinced of total infallibility in everything as to put principles into practice with a godlike unconcern for everybody else. It would, however, be a great tragedy if monks, who are in possession of the highest religious truth, failed to serve it with the generosity and zeal which are shown by some Communists in the service of error.

Finally, and most important, Communism is rowing with the stream, and since we are living in an age of chaotic change, it is much easier to destroy than to support what has been standing for centuries. It is consequently quite easy for Communism to predict victories and achieve them — since they are almost entirely destructive. Each "victory" sweeps into the fold of Communism new millions of under-privileged people who have little or nothing to lose by the change, since they have nothing in the first place. It is an easy matter to enlist their enthusiastic support and to instil into them a conviction that they are really "getting somewhere." Working on these millions, giving them a sense of achievement and self-liberation, through astute propaganda, the Reds can easily create and form a whole new world of Communists, and surround us with an accomplished fact. The internal problems within Communism itself will make themselves all too evident later, for even more than Capitalism, Communism contains within itself the seeds of its own decay. But as long as it is merely a matter of tearing down the established order, and seizing power, Communism is a most formidable opponent.

What is the position for the monk in the presence of this great destructive drive?

First of all, it should be clear that the monk is placed, by his vocation itself, beyond and outside politics. In so far as he is a monk, he has no direct, active part to play in the political drama. If he is dragged on to the stage, it can only be by violence, and precisely in order that he may bear witness to the God whom politics ignores, or treats with an abstract or formal respect at best. In so far as he is a citizen of a human state, the monk does, of course, avail himself of his privileges and exercise his responsibilities — but here he is no longer acting precisely as a monk — and in fact he no longer uses his monastic name on these occasions.

But in the second place, it is clear that totalitarian dictatorships do not permit the existence, within the state, of groups dedicated to any reality which claims to be above the state. If Communism ever tolerated the monk, he would have to be in some sense a "stooge" of the Red dictatorship, and this is incompatible with a true monastic vocation. As soon as the monk identifies himself completely with the temporal interests and aims of any merely human society, he puts himself in the "service of corruption" as St. Paul would say. That is, he leaves what is spiritual, supernatural, and everlasting in order to embrace what is doomed to decay and pass from the scene.

However, it is clear that the monk is in fact, and by the very nature of things, bound to associate himself with a society that has an ideal in some way akin to his own. His fate is, therefore, bound up with that of the free democracies at the present time.

In making their cause his own, the monk recognizes whatever is truly his own, because truly Christian, in the democratic ideal. That is to say that, passing over the love of ease and wealth and the doctrine of materialistic *laissez faire,* the monk defends the democratic ideal of freedom not by talking about it but by living it on the highest spiritual plane. The monk aids democracy by elevating freedom to the level of divine charity and self-sacrifice — the "Law of Liberty" which is the Law of God Himself. The monastery remains, then a center of spiritual freedom, from which radiates the power of divine grace, and the liberty of the Holy Ghost. The unity in charity which prevails in the monastic community clearly but silently reproduces on earth the divine exemplar, of which all other human freedoms are a less definite shadow.

The monk should not imagine that in a chaotic age like ours his only function is to preserve the ancient attitudes and customs of his Order. These are necessary and valuable indeed in so far as they are vital and fruitful, and help us to live more freely and more consciously in the Mystery of Christ. The past should live on, and the monk is indeed a preserver of the past. However, the monastery should be something more than a museum. If the monk *merely* keeps in existence monuments of literature and art and thought that would otherwise decay, he is not what he ought to be. He will decay with what is decaying all around him.

The monk does not, in fact, exist to preserve anything, be it even contemplation or religion itself. His function is not to keep alive in the world the memory of God. God depends on no one to live and act in the world, not even on His monks! On the contrary, the function of the monk in our time is to *keep himself alive by contact with God.*

While all the rest of the world bows down before money, power, and science, the monk spurns worldly expedients and gives himself in poverty, humility and faith to the Almighty. While all the rest of the world adores the machine and engages in a frenzied cult of work for its own sake, the monk, while living by the labor of his hands, remembers that man's highest and most fruitful activity is the spiritual "work" of contemplation. While the world, enslaved by its own material needs and desires, drives itself mad with anxiety, the monk rises above anguish to dwell in peace in the "Sabbath" of divine charity.

In our age in which everyone else is carried away with the exigencies of a great cultural and political struggle, the monk has, as his primary function, the duty to *be a monk* — to be a man of God, that is to say, a man who lives by and for God alone. Only by doing this can the monk preserve what is rich and vital in his monastic and Christian tradition.

In order to be what he is meant to be, the monk must rise above the common ethical level of humanitarian paganism, and live the "theological" life centred on God, a life of pure faith, of hope in God's providence, of charity in the Holy Spirit. He must live in the "Mystery of Christ." He must see that Christ and His Church are one, and he must center his whole life in this one faith and one direction, to the unity of the One Church of Christ.

In the darkness of the struggle, the monk must cling with all the powers of his soul to the teachings of the Church, to the authority and sanctifying power of the Church. He cannot depend on his own limited vision, or make crucial decisions on the basis of his own judgment. Now above all he must think and act with the Church.

In short — the monk's vocation at all times is to live in, and for, and by Christ. But most especially when the Mystery of iniquity works most openly in the world, it is necessary for the monk to dissociate himself from all that is not spiritual and Christian, from all that tends to anything but God, in order to keep alive in the world that spiritual atmosphere without which all that is good and sane in human culture will die of asphyxiation.

In the night of our technological barbarism, monks must be as trees which exist silently in the dark, and by their vital presence purify the air.